HOW TO WRITE A PROFESSIONAL RESUME

Written By: April Jackson

The trademarks that are used are without any consent, and the publication of the trademark is without permission or backing by the trademark owner. All trademarks and brands within this book are for clarifying purposes only and are the owned by the owners themselves, not affiliated with this document.

Disclaimer and Terms of Use: The Author and Publisher has strived to be as accurate and complete as possible in the creation of this book, notwithstanding the fact that he does not warrant or represent at any time that the contents within are accurate due to the rapidly changing nature of the Internet. While all attempts have been made to verify information provided in this publication, the Author and Publisher assumes no responsibility for errors, omissions, or contrary interpretation of the subject matter herein.

Any perceived slights of specific persons, peoples, or organizations are unintentional. In practical advice books, like anything else in life, there are no guarantees of results. Readers are cautioned to rely on their own judgment about their individual circumstances and act accordingly.

This book is not intended for use as a source of legal, medical, business, accounting or financial advice. All readers are advised to seek services of competent professionals in the legal, medical, business, accounting, and finance fields.

Table of Contents

Introduction

Let's face it. Writing a resume is a daunting task. While the resources providing writing tips are many, few actually provide a step by step process on how to write one. If you want to write it on your own, I commend your courage.

 For most people writing a good resume is tough. It takes time. The worst part comes when you finally think that you have a great resume, but you're still not getting interviews. You can make your resume as pleasing as possible to the average hiring manager by following some commonly accepted guidelines.

Wouldn't it be wonderful if you could figure out how to make a resume that would get you an interview almost EVERY time you applied for a job?

This eBook will be your guide to a professional resume that can land you the job of your dreams.

Hiring managers only spend around 15 seconds scanning over a new resume. They are really only looking for a couple of things. They're sort of on autopilot. Hiring managers would like to know these basic things:

1) Who have you worked for?
2) Have you had steady employment?
3) What notable achievements and recognitions have you attained throughout your career?
4) What do you have to offer that will meet with their specific needs?

An effective resume will answer the previously stated questions with a minimal amount of effort. As with any effective marketing tool, it will also leave the hiring manager wanting to know more. You want to give them just enough info to prompt them into action. That's when they pick up the phone and call you for an interview!

Your resume is your professional introduction. It's your only chance to make a memorable first impression. I can tell you right now that if you do not take your resume seriously, your resume will never be TAKEN seriously. It's really that simple.

Now, if you feel you are capable and □ualified to write a compelling and dynamic resume, then by all means give it a shot. However, if you're not extremely confident in your skills as a writer, I would sincerely recommend you take this eBook very seriously.

For those who are convinced they have what it takes, this should also help you with some of the finer points. Although job markets and technologies are always changing, there are some things which are fairly universal and constitute the basic principles of a winning resume. To guide you along, I have compiled this eBook with secret tricks of the trade as well as a collection of common mistakes people make. So pay close attention. Take my advice into consideration. Then you will be on your way to landing that dream job in no time!

How to Write your Professional Resume

Can you possibly land that dream job with a professional resume?

You sure can if you follow the process that I am about to share with you step-by-step. BEST of all, this resume writing process is quick and will land you interviews.

Here's what you're going to find:

* How to write a resume for a job with examples for every section.
* Quick but little-known tips to follow to get up to 10x MORE INTERVIEWS.
* Answers to all of your questions about how to make the best resume for a job.

* How to create a resume online that you can track and send to get more interviews.
* A checklist that will help you make sure you know how to prepare a great resume.

This is what you need to do, to write a resume that gets you the job:

1. Decide Whether You Need a Resume or a CV

What is a resume?

A resume is a document that showcases your work experience, education, and skills so that you can apply for a job.

What's the difference between a resume and a CV?

Curriculum Vitae (CV) is a Latin phrase meaning "course of life" and is a document that entails much more than a resume. Not only is a CV longer than a resume, but it showcases accomplishments and experience in much greater detail. It's the ideal document for academics.

Once you know if you should write a CV or resume, it's time to choose the right format.

2. Choose the Right Resume Format to Stand Out

What does a resume look like?

There are three types of professional resume formats:

* Chronological (or Reverse-Chronological)
* Combination (or Hybrid)
* Functional (or Skills-Based)

Most job seekers choose the reverse-chronological resume format.

Resume Format

1. Reverse-chronological

Pros

* Traditional
* Familiar to Recruiters

Cons

* Common
* Not Creative

2. Combination

Pros

* Experienced professionals can highlight skills.
* Career changers can emphasize transferrable skills.

Cons

* Uncommon and not as familiar to recruiters.
* Not suggested for entry-level job seekers.

3. Functional or "Skills-based"

Pros

* Entry-level job seekers can emphasize skills instead of experience.

Cons

* Recruiters may think you're hiding something.

Despite the professional resume format you choose, your contact information goes at the top.

Here is how to write a resume contact section:

Contact Information
Your Name
Phone Number
Professional Email Address
Social Media Handles (Twitter and LinkedIn)
URLs to Personal Websites or Blogs

Adding your address is optional. It is no longer necessary to add it to a modern resume. Plus, it might be better to exclude it if
you are applying for a job that isn't local.

Your email address should be professional which means:

* Choosing a sophisticated email provider.

RIGHT   **WRONG**
johnsmith@gmail.com   johnsmith@hotmail.com

* Not using your current work email. Instead, create a professional, private email address.

* Avoiding email addresses from when you were in high school. It won't amuse recruiters to see johnlikesgoats@hotmail.com or sexysara@gmail.com. Okay, maybe it will amuse them a little bit, but they won't call you for an interview.

RIGHT   **WRONG**
johnsmith@gmail.com   johnlikesgoats@hotmail.com

Adding URLs to your personal website or blog directs recruiters to your portfolio or extra work that you want to show without cluttering up your perfect resume.

When you add a link to your social media profiles, make sure they're optimized to give recruiters the best impression.

4. Start Your Resumes Like the Best Candidates Do

Again, what does a resume look like? Well, you know that contact information comes first. But what comes next? Education? Experience?

Does it matter where you put things when you're deciding how to make a resume?

The short answer is yes, it does matter. That's because your best stuff should go in the top third of your resume.

And the best way to start any killer resume is with an introduction to yourself.

Think of it like this:

The top of your resume is the penthouse. It's the most important piece of real estate on the document. But why?

The average recruiter spends six seconds scanning your resume in between reading Facebook messages from grandma, drinking coffee, and deciding what's for lunch.

The recruiter is looking for very specific information which the recruiter will only look for it in the top third of your resume. If you do not grab the recruiters attention, game over.

This is why a creative resume summary or objective can save the day.

What is a resume summary statement?

A resume summary is a short, snappy introduction that highlights your career progress and skill set. It should also demonstrate why you'll be a valuable hire.

Example Resume Summary:

Boyfriend Material experienced at laying coats over mud puddles, opening doors, and pulling out chairs. Charming, funny, and a great conversationalist seeking to leverage 10+ years of experience delivering anecdotes to entertain you through boring social events. Has an MA in hand holding and a license to cook romantic dinners.

What is a resume objective statement?

A resume objective achieves the same thing as a resume summary. The difference is how you write one and who should use it.

Example Resume Objective:

Experienced Chef interested in becoming a Zoo Keeper. Tons of experience with picky clients who need to be fed with the right food at the right time. Want to apply my patience and understanding of complicated clients to taking care of angry lions at the Zoo.

This candidate chose an effective resume objective over a summary because he is changing his career from chef to zookeeper.

Either way, the point is to focus on the employer's needs and not your own.

Who should use an objective for a resume?

1. Entry-level Applicants and Students
2. Career Changers

3. Professionals Targeting Specific Positions

You can also choose to write something called a professional profile.
A good resume profile lists your □ualifications, experience, and education
regarding the company's needs and values. It can be formatted as a
paragraph or as a list with resume bullet points.

5. Write a Resume Experience Section That Will Get You More Job Offers

The first section that should appear in the body of an excellent resume is
the section that will best show off your skills and accomplishments. For
most of you, that will probably be the experience section. Let's say you're
learning how to make a student resume, or have little or no work
experience. In that case, lead with your education or skills section.

But do you know how to write a resume employment history? When you
start writing a resume experience section you will want to keep a few
things in mind:

* Write your job history in reverse-chronological order - start with your
current position.
* Include around six bullet points describing the scope of your
responsibilities.
* Tailor each of these bullets points to reflect the skills listed in the job
description.
* Follow the bullet point format (see below), and include facts and figures.
* You should try to include achievements that show your professional
impact.
* Tell a career story that reinforces your professinal persona.

Sample Resume Experience Entry:

RIGHT

Marketing Manager 2014 - Present
ABC Company, Albany, NY

* Spearhead a global brand strategy for our top performing product.
Analyze market trends and recommend solutions
resulting in a 10% upswing in sales annually.
* Prepare Portfolio Deployment Plans.
* Head up a team of 10+ marketing specialists.

WRONG

Marketing Manager 2014 - Present
ABC Company, Albany, NY
* Organize marketing materials.
Responsible for brand strategy.
Responsible for analyzing market trends.

Responsible for a team of marketing specialists.

Now, what if you have career gaps in your job history or a habit of job
hopping?

Let's face it. Not all of us have a squeaky clean job history. It's difficult to
know how to create a resume that addresses career gaps without cheating.

One approach is to include a brief explanation next to each job.

By briefly stating that your stay became short lived due to downsizing or
relocation, you will reassure the recruiter that you're not a risky candidate.
Chronic career hoppers may be tempted to tamper with dates, leaving only
the years in their experience section:

RIGHT	**WRONG**
October 2005 - January 2006	2005 - 2006

Excluding the months makes it look like you worked a year instead of three
months. But it's a dirty trick that employers know well, which makes it a big
no, no.

Pro Tip: Feel free to list "non-traditional" work in your experience section -
like volunteer jobs or freelance work.

6. Prepare an Education Section Which Adds More Value Than Others

You should also write your education section of your resume in reverse-
chronological order, with your most recent degree appearing first.

Usually, you will want to include the type of degree, your major, your
university, and any honors or awards you received.

You can skip your GPA. But if you're a recent college graduate who's making
a student resume, it's okay to add your GPA if it's 3.5 or higher.

You can also include a coursework narrative. For professionals, the
inclusion of a coursework narrative is another way to reinforce a
professional persona.

7. Focus On Your Skills Section to Increase Your Interview Chances

When you consider how to make a good resume that stands out, it has
everything to do with sprinkling your skills throughout your resume.

But, it also makes sense to have a big section labeled "SKILLS."

Use the key skills listed in the job description. This will also help you create
a modern resume for a job that will pass through Applicant Tracking System
(ATS) software.

Recruiters should be able to see two things when they look at your skills for
a resume:

1. You have the skill set they want and re□uested in the job post.
2. You have extra skills that prove you are a valuable worker.

RIGHT
MS Excel - Advanced (Macros, Pivot Tables)
WRONG
Has a great command of MS Excel.

8. Add Additional Resume Sections to Stand Out from the Rest

Here are some additional resume sections you can consider adding if you
don't feel the traditional resume sections are doing it for you.

* Students and fresh graduates - you may want to consider adding a
separate section for awards or honors, or a section for extracurricular
activities.
* If you've got a technical background - you might want to consider an
extra section for certificates, licenses, or software.
* Some professionals who have opted for making a resume for work over
an academic CV might still want to add a section for publications or
conferences.
* Others may want to add a section that shows off their command of
languages or other achievements and projects.

Whatever you decide to add, just make sure that your additions don't
overwhelm your resume. You still want everything to fit onto one page if
possible.

9. Include a Hobbies & Interests Section to Show You're a Great Fit

The hobbies section of a resume is optional. But, I recommend adding one
if you have space. Adding your interests shows off extra skills for a resume,
makes your resume stand out, and gives the hiring manager a fuller
image of you. Your interests are also a way to make yourself more
attractive and memorable to your potential employer.

You can always cut this section later if your resume is too long.

RIGHT	**WRONG**
Reading Russian Literature	Reading

10. Tailor Your Resume to the Job Description to Get the Best Job Offers

On average, a corporate job offer attracts up to 250 resumes. Of those, 4 to 6 candidates will get invited for an interview. Only one person will get the job.

With so many resumes to sift through, recruiters are using something called Applicant Tracking System (ATS) software.

The software compares your resume to the job description based on resume keywords. In order to prepare a resume that will make it through ATS you will need to tailor your resume.

Tailoring a resume to the job description is adding resume keywords and information from the job offer.

For starters, you're going to want to make a master resume.

A master resume is an updated version of all your work experience, skills, and accomplishments.

When you sit down to write a tailored version of your resume, you will pick and choose material from your master resume to match the specific job for which you are applying.

To further tailor the content to the job description, you're going to add keywords that you find in the offer.

Let's say you want to apply for a job as a copywriter.

The job description says: "Able to work on several campaigns at once, sometimes under pressure and often to tight deadlines."

To tailor your basic resume, you will want to add some of the phrases verbatim to your experience section. For example: "Work on several campaigns at once."

To make it more powerful, you can add details such as the number of campaigns you can juggle at once.

RIGHT
Juggle up to 4 campaigns at once often to tight deadlines.

WRONG
Work on several campaigns at once.

11. Show, Don't Tell - Here's How to Include Achievements for the Win

If you're struggling with how to make a good resume stand out, all you need to do is make things quantifiable wherever possible. Using numbers gives the recruiter some tangible proof of an achievement.

Here are some basic resume examples of achievements:

RIGHT
Increased sales by 15% by renegotiating a key account contract in the first month of employment.

WRONG
Significantly increased sales.

RIGHT
Proficient use of MS Excel (pivot tables and macros).

WRONG
MS Excel.

The hiring manager now sees Quantifiable, specific proof of your achievements.

12. Add Achievements to Show Why You're the Best Match

Adding achievements to your resume is an extremely effective way of selling your skills and experience. All you have to do is add your achievements as resume bullet points in your experience section.

You will want to use the PAR (Problem Action Result) Approach to writing your achievements:

Here are a few right and wrong resume examples of how to write achievements:

Problem: My previous employer wanted to increase revenue.

Action: I created a new marketing campaign on Facebook.

Result: We saw an increase in sales by 15% and an increase in revenue by 10%.

RIGHT
Increased revenue by 10% and sales by 15% by implementing a marketing campaign on Facebook.

WRONG
Increased sales and revenue through social media marketing techniques.

13. Replace Boring Words with Action Words - Here's How

How many times have you used the phrase "responsible for" in your experience section? You may want to consider mixing up your vocabulary. Overusing words and phrases like "responsible for" or "manage" is boring.

Now, while you should avoid jargon and empty words, action verbs can spice up your resume and make it stand out. Also, be sure to use the present tense when describing your current role.

Here are a few before and after resume examples:

RIGHT	WRONG
Orchestrated	Managed
Negotiated	Communicated
Overhauled	Innovated

Negotiated a streamlined approach to the internal use of Salesforce among project leaders. Overhauled external marketing materials for Continental Europe across all markets.

Pro Tip: Don't overdo it. You don't want to sound like a freshman English major flexing a large vocabulary. Avoid resume buzzwords like "synergy."

14. Show Your Career Progression to Prove You're the Right Candidate

What makes a good resume? CEO, Director, Manager - all you need is a big, impressive title, right?

Not exactly.

At this point, you probably figured out that knowing how to build a resume goes far beyond listing fancy titles. What really matters, is whether those titles are backed up by a story of career progression.

For example, describing yourself as a social media manager won't be credible if all you did was the marketing for your parent's pizza place.

You have to show a steady progression into a management position. Each former role should reinforce your place in the next one.

Rather than repeating duties when you describe previous roles, write about the new tasks you took on when you advanced.

Marketing

Marketing Manager:

* Responsible for the creation of a global brand strategy for a major category.
* Prepare Category and Portfolio Deployment Plans.
* Analyze market trends and recommend solutions.
* Team Management (10 marketing specialists).

Marketing Specialist / Senior Marketing Specialist:

* Planned and implemented promotional campaigns.
* Cooperated with interactive agencies.
* Managed project budgets and timeline control.

Marketing Intern:

* Researched information.
* Assisted during promotional campaigns.

15. Draw Attention to Promotions to Stand Out from the Crowd - Here's How

Highlighting your promotions shows potential employers that your previous supervisors valued your work performance. Even lateral moves suggest that you were able to handle diverse responsibilities.

Here are a few ways to describe your promotions while writing a resume:

Repeatedly recognized for top performance through fast-track promotions and selection for high-priority initiatives. Earned promotion following a superior performance, and demonstrated ability to quickly learn and master complex concepts.

What if you moved up within the same organization?

You don't have to mention the name of the same company more than once. It will make even the best resume look messy.

Here's what to do instead:

COMPANY NAME – City, State, 2001 to Present

* Store Manager January 2005 to Present
Describe responsibilities and achievements.

* Assistant Manager January 2002 to January 2005
Describe responsibilities and achievements.

* Clerk January 2001 to January 2002
Describe responsibilities and achievements.

16. Make Your Resume Easy to Read - A Quick Tip

Need to know how to make a resume easy for a recruiter to read? It's as simple as aligning your text to the left.

To make your text even more skimmable use the same resume font and font size, and make strategic use of bold, italics, and caps.

The bulk of your resume will consist of bullet points. Here's how to construct them:

Action Verb + Quantifiable Point + Specific Task

Spearheaded a targeted email campaign that resulted in a 15% upswing in newsletter registration.

You might also want to consider how to create a resume using templates. Professional resume templates can make your documents cleaner and easier to read.

They also save you time and energy. Let's face it. No one likes trying to control one-inch margins in Word.

17. Choose the Best Font So Your Resume Reads Well

While choosing a basic resume font may seem like a silly chore - it's not. A good font will ensure that your resume is readable.

What is the best font for a resume?

The best font for a resume is one that a recruiter can read with no effort.

Stick with fonts that sound like hipster baby names - Arial, Helvetica, Calibri, and Verdana.

What is the best resume font size?

The Goldilocks font size is 10-12 points - not too big and not too small. Keep it uniform.

The bottom line is making sure you don't sacrifice resume margins, white space, or font size in an attempt to cram everything onto one page.

RIGHT   **WRONG**
Arial Comic   Sans

18. Save Your Resume the Right Way - Follow These Steps

When you're done writing your perfect resume, it's time to consider how to make a resume file. That's not as obvious as it
sounds.

 The best advice is to save your resume as a PDF and give it your name.

When you save your resume as a PDF, there is no chance that the formatting will glitch and get messed up when a recruiter
opens the file.

Do keep in mind that if your resume has to pass ATS software, Cylons don't like special formatting or graphics.

Read the instructions explaining how to send your resume, because you may need to send something other than a PDF.

How should you name your files?

RIGHT   **WRONG**
Your Name Resume   Resume1

For example:

"Han Solo Resume"

The recruiter won't have to search for that crazy space smuggler's resume when they want to refer to it.

19. Keep Your Resume Short - Here's An Easy Way

How long should an ideal resume be?

Or, more specifically, should a resume be one page?

Most contemporary resume guidelines will tell you that while making a resume, you should do your best to keep it to a single page.

But will a 2-page resume crush your chances? Not necessarily. You don't want to keep relevant experience off your resume. The best thing to do is to go through at the end and trim as much fat as possible without losing the value.

Here are three tips on how to make a resume for a job shorter:

* Trim introductions.
* Cut extra bullet points. (6 or less)
* Kill or trim the additional sections. (Hobbies)

If you aren't sure how long your resume should be or need more advice on how to make a resume shorter, read our guide:

How Long Should a Resume Be? Ideal Resume Length (+Tips)

20. Use Proofreading Tools to Make Your Resume Error-Free in 5 Minutes

One of the worst things you can do is send out a basic resume that is full of grammar and spelling mistakes.

You need to proofread your resume.

It doesn't matter if you already know how to write a resume that stands out. Even the best resumes need to be proofread by a second person.

Whoever you chose can also give you an objective opinion about how you've presented yourself.

Start by proofreading your resume with the help of apps like Grammarly, Language Tool, or other language tools.

Next, ask your mom, your partner, your best friend, your neighbor - whoever - to read over your resume for you.

21. Clean Up Your Online Image to Improve Your Interview Chances

Before sending your resume, you will want to check your online presence. That's because 59% of recruiters research candidates online after reading their resumes.

Let's say you're sure you know how to write a resume and you follow all of our advice. That won't matter if you skip this step.

Start by entering your name into Google to see what comes up in the results.

Most of you will find links to your social media profiles. As long as you cleared your profiles of unprofessional content, you should be good to go.

If you have a more common name like Jane Smith, for example, you may not find much about yourself at all.

Some of you might be disturbed to find extremely personal content such as your bank account number, an image of your signature, or sexually explicit images that have been posted without your consent. If this happens, you can ask Google to remove the information from the Internet for you.

If you find some embarrassing content on a web page, Google suggests that it is best to contact the webmaster (owner) to have the image or content removed.

22. Write a Cover Letter - Here's Why It's a Must

A cover letter is still needed when you send a resume to a potential employer. Up to 45% of recruiters will reject resumes without cover letters.

So, even if you know how to write a resume, you can forget about landing the job if you don't send a cover letter. Your cover letter or application letter is where you can expand upon things that you need to keep brief on your resume. It also needs to be tailored to the job for which you are applying.

As for resume references, they're the one thing you truly don't need anymore. So, lose the phrase "references upon request." Plus, a great cover letter that match your resume will give you an advantage over other candidates.

23. Send a Personal Message to be Better than 9 Candidates out of 10

When you send your resume to a general email address like jobs@company.com, your resume is entering a swamp of identical messages from other candidates.

One thing you can do to differentiate your message is to try to find out the name of the person who will be reading your resume and send them a personal email.

This is not the best solution in every case. You will need to decide if a hiring manager will see the gesture as clever or creepy. Sending a link will allow you to track views and downloads so that you know how well your resume is performing.

24. Find Out If the Employer Read Your Resume - Here's How

Once you've sent your resume, it's a good idea to track it. You can install a free sales tool like Mixmax or YesWare to help you.

Knowing if recruiters have opened and read your email will enable you to follow-up on your job application promptly or find different email addresses.

Key Takeaway

Your resume is your passport to job interviews. Knowing how to make a resume for a job is the first step on any career path.

Take the time and energy to think about how to write a resume well and how to tailor it to the job description. If you can do that, you're well on your way to the next level - the interview.

Conclusion

Resumes are critically important in your job search and can even make the difference between success and failure. Following the above guidelines will help ensure that you go to the job market with a good resume that outshines those of your competitors. Still, this is not a time to skimp and cut corners. Take every detail in this eBook very seriously and you will achieve success. While this is an investment, it is an investment that will almost surely pay you back many times over.